President Polk said in 1848 that if California was left without a government for another year, "it might be lost to the Union . . . they would probably organize an independent government, calling it the California or Pacific Republic." Military rule lingered, for Congress had not given California a government because of the slavery issue. So Californians decided to organize a provincial government. A convention met in Monterey in September, 1849, and a constitution stating that slavery would never be tolerated was signed on October 14. The "best legis-

" fol- were to go to Washington, where they urged that California be admitted immediately to the Union. They were opposed by Calhoun: two new senators from a free state bothered southerners. He predicted civil war. Still, the Senate passed a bill for admission and the House passed it, too. It was approved on September 9. On October 18, a beflagged steamer, the *Oregon*, sailed through the Golden Gate with a banner which said CALIFORNIA IS A STATE. Guns boomed, and the flag, with another star of paper pinned on was run up on the lofty staff. . ."

The Grand Celebration
October 29, 1850
OF CALIFORNIA'S ADMISSION
TO THE UNION,
September 9, 1850

Sources:
lithographs by C. Pollard, F. Marryatt and S.F. newspapers, etc.

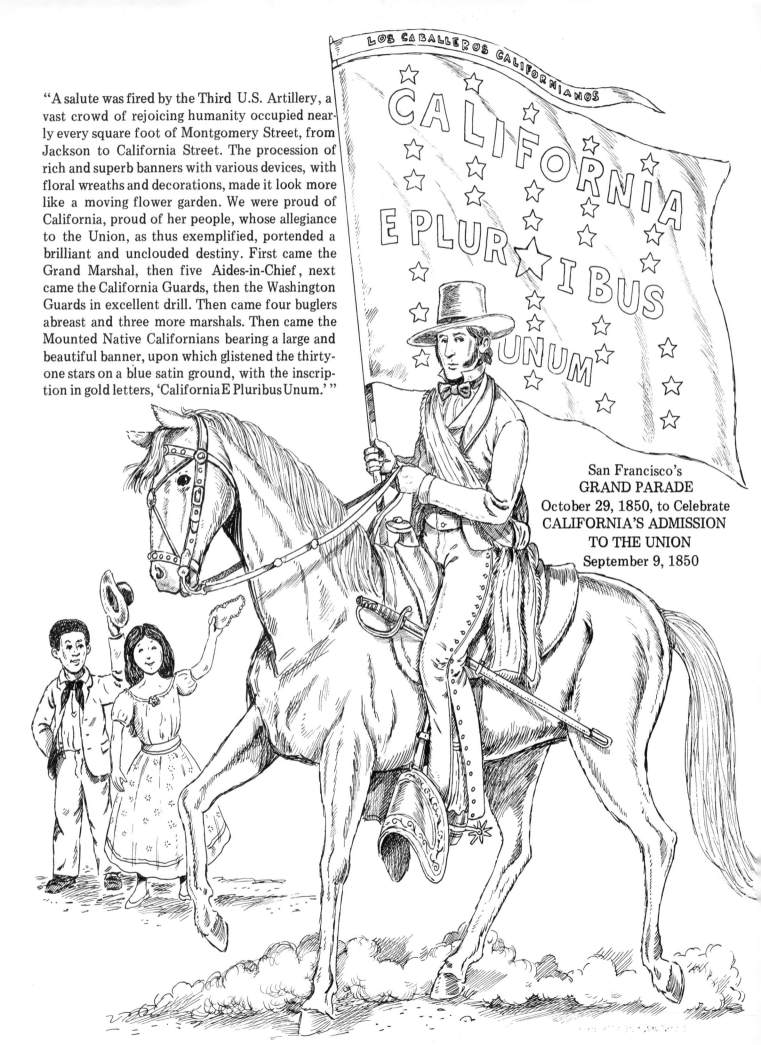

"A salute was fired by the Third U.S. Artillery, a vast crowd of rejoicing humanity occupied nearly every square foot of Montgomery Street, from Jackson to California Street. The procession of rich and superb banners with various devices, with floral wreaths and decorations, made it look more like a moving flower garden. We were proud of California, proud of her people, whose allegiance to the Union, as thus exemplified, portended a brilliant and unclouded destiny. First came the Grand Marshal, then five Aides-in-Chief, next came the California Guards, then the Washington Guards in excellent drill. Then came four buglers abreast and three more marshals. Then came the Mounted Native Californians bearing a large and beautiful banner, upon which glistened the thirty-one stars on a blue satin ground, with the inscription in gold letters, 'California E Pluribus Unum.'"

LOS CABALLEROS CALIFORNIANOS

CALIFORNIA
E PLURIBUS UNUM

San Francisco's
GRAND PARADE
October 29, 1850, to Celebrate
**CALIFORNIA'S ADMISSION
TO THE UNION**
September 9, 1850

Then came the Society of California Pioneers, with this beautiful banner painted with the State Seal with Minerva, goddess of industry and good government, in the center, presiding over the building of the state. She encourages the arts and protects the home. Keep at it, old girl. Then came the officers of the Army and Navy followed by officers and soldiers of the New York Volunteers. Next were the Orators representatives of foreign governments, Frémont Battalion and First Regiment of of the Day, Clergymen, consuls and and Queen Victoria's subjects.

A youth, who bore,
'mid snow and ice,
A banner, with
the strange device,
Excelsior!
- *Longfellow*

A PRELUDE CELEBRATION, JULY 4, '49

At Sea Aboard the Fast Sailing Ship *Sutton*, (which had left New York on Jan. 1, 1849 and would arrive at San Francisco 18 days after this scene). Celebrations were grand affairs in the last century, for they had no TV then to amuse folks and make them lazy. Many '49ers were still *en route* to California when our national day came that year. This allowed them, nonetheless, practice at celebrating our glorious, expanding Union with its great new land: California! Here is one small celebration on the high Pacific Ocean, a prelude to the grand celebration which would take place the following year when California became a state. "At the command of: 'Company, Three paces in the rear, March,' some came forward, breaking the ranks and presenting a very Straggling appearance; the troops took up the line of march and passed in review. The Captain complimented the Commanding officer upon the orderly appearance and equipment of (the) men: a Continental pioneer bearing a large broad ax; a harlequin, his pants & Shirt being one-half blue, and the other half red, one Side of his face was black, and the other side red; a tatterdemalion; an overgrown boy from the Country, with jacket too Small to button, and pants reaching just below the knees; old 'Seventy-Sixers,' (one) wearing an enomous wig made of manilla rope; and an Ensign, neatly and appropriately equipped bearing a Small American flag with the motto, 'Excelsior.' The remainder of the corps were as fantastically dressed, the whole group presenting a fit Subject of mirth. Having passed in review, they were drawn up in a line upon the lee-board Side of the vessel, when a Second Salute of 13 guns was fired. The Stars & Stripes was being raised to the peak at the Same time, amidst the loud acclamations of every soul on board ... Then was Sung the National Anthem, 'Hail Columbia ...' The next exercise was an oration: Our land is a paradisical refuge for the oppressed of the world ... They are all welcomed, our continent is amply large for as many as choose to come."

Text: Journal of T.Whaley, edited by J.Reading, Whaley House, San Diego, 1972.
Excelsior was the motto of New York, and the subject of a poem by Longfellow, 1841.

In a Chinese hotel in San Francisco a little later, "the proprietor took us into his private room, and showed us a flag he had received from home; it was twenty feet long and twelve broad of the nicest crape, crimson, the design an immense dragon, wrought with gold thread, the same on both sides. . . with enormous eyes gazing at the moon, and some Chinese figures, making the most magnificent thing of the kind I ever saw, but there is no place in the world but this where there is wind enough to float such an extensive affair."
—Letter of Mary Megguier, May 30, 1852, Huntington Library

"The Chinese appeared in their rich native costume, presenting a fine appearance, with an elegant blue banner.* The triumphal car came next, with thirty boys representing the thirty states, each with the national arms with the name of a state. Then in the center of this magnificent car appeared a smiling little girl, dressed in white with gold and silver gauze floating gracefully from her head. She held a shield upon which was inscribed: 'California—the Union, it must and shall be preserved.' Then came the mayor, recorder, aldermen and judicial officers of the city, with a large banner inscribed: 'San Francisco—The Commercial Emporium of the Pacific.' Next came the police department, with an elegant blue satin banner surmounted with a golden eagle, inscribed 'San Francisco Police Department—Semper Paratus.' "

* "In 1850 at the celebration in San Francisco of the admission of California into the Union, the Chinese were given the post of honor. . . and placed directly after the state and city officials in the long line," wrote farmer Stuart of Sonoma twenty-seven years later. "It was their labor that made California what it was. It was their men . . . that had mainly built the railroads, cleared the farms, reclaimed a million acres of swamp and overflowed land, planted the orchards and vineyards, reaped the crops and gathered the fruits, dug and sacked the potatoes, manufactured the woolen and other goods, cleaned up the tailings of the hydraulic mines, scraped the bed-rock of the exhausted placers, built the cities. . . Nearly everything of value had been done by them."-Hittell, *History of California*, v.4, 622-3

After a lithograph of Cooke & Le Count, 1852

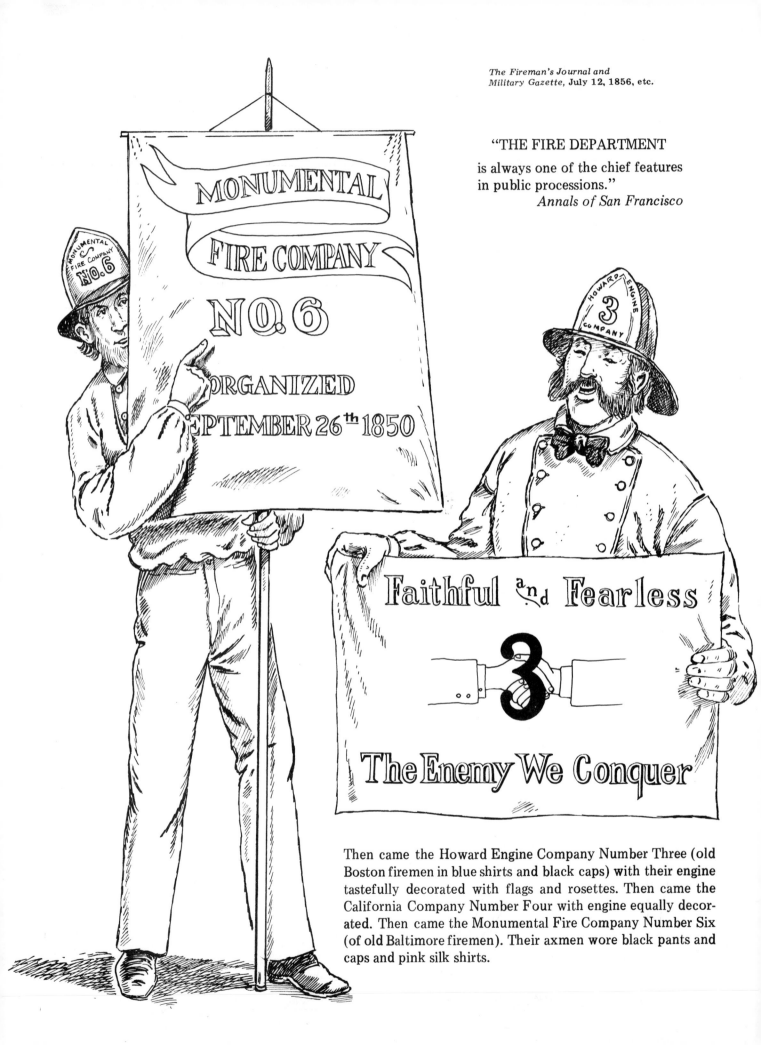

The Fireman's Journal and Military Gazette, July 12, 1856, etc.

"THE FIRE DEPARTMENT
is always one of the chief features
in public processions."
Annals of San Francisco

Then came the Howard Engine Company Number Three (old Boston firemen in blue shirts and black caps) with their engine tastefully decorated with flags and rosettes. Then came the California Company Number Four with engine equally decorated. Then came the Monumental Fire Company Number Six (of old Baltimore firemen). Their axmen wore black pants and caps and pink silk shirts.

Then came the Saint Francis Hook and Ladder Company, with a richly trimmed blue satin banner inscribed "We destroy to save." In the years 1850, '51 and '52, the principal work at fires fell to the hook and ladder companies because it was impossible to obtain water for the engines . . . Soon after came the Knickerbocker Engine Company Number Five—red shirts and black caps. The San Francisco fire department was set in motion on Christmas, 1849, the day after the first great fire. David C. Broderick and other old New York firemen were among the founders. Their fire companies had been used to disputing by fist fights the honor of putting out fires. Broderick became foreman of the Empire Engine Company Number One, also a fighting political organization. He soon after became U.S. Senator from California, a fierce anti-slavery Democrat when President Buchanan's Democracy was pro-slavery, and when southerners controlled California. He was killed in a duel for this; then did California sentiment switch towards getting rid of that vile institution and staying with the Union.

The Knickerbocker Banner was presented by John Hoxie, amidst "the genial old Dutch hospitality." *The Fireman's Journal and Military Gazette,* October 16, 1856

The Dutch flag of Old New Amsterdam: top stripe orange red, middle white, bottom blue

Next came the Sansome Hook and Ladder Company Number Three, wearing red shirts and black pants and caps. They were always in charge of the powder magazine for blowing up buildings at fires. Their carriage was decked in magnificent style, with five banners as shown here. Over the carriage was formed a pyramid of short ladders, decked with flowers, upon which perched a live American eagle. The pyramid seemed to form an appropriate arbor for "The Belle of the Pacific," a most beautiful little lass of some eight or ten years of age, said to have been the first child born of American parents in California. The air resounded with huzzas whenever "the Belle" made her appearance.

SANSOME HOOK and LADDER COMPANY NO. 3

ORGANIZED JUNE 14, 1850

WE RAZE TO SAVE

A TREASU FOUNI

LAFAYETTE

HOOK and LADDER

CIE. NO.

2

SAN FRANCISCO

CALIFORNIE

Next came the boatmen with a decorated boat, with banners inscribed "United we pull a more effective Stroke," "By Commerce we Thrive," "In Union we pull Together." Then came a car of the Pacific Topographical Society upon which was the first printing press made in California, printing for the crowds Mrs. Wills's Ode:

> Rejoice! Hear ye not o'er the hills of the East
> The sound of our welcome to Liberty's Union?
> Pledge high! for we join in the mystical feast
> That our forefathers hallowed at Freedom's communion!
>
> . . .
>
> And the Band of the Union, oh, long may it be
> The hope of th'oppressed and the shield of the free!

It was sung to the tune of the 'Star Spangled Banner.' Many more followed in the parade, and afterwards there were ceremonies at the plaza. All the bands together played 'Hail Columbia' and then the 'Marseillaise,' for there were many Frenchmen in California, and it was the French who had helped our country of liberty at its birth. Afterwards cannon boomed again, small arms fired, firecrackers banged, and fireworks lit up the evening. It was a glorious day to celebrate an event for which we too are happy.

AND THE YANKEES FOLLOWED ...

The joyful news of free gold had gladdened the Yankee heart; few young men were left at home in 1849. Most came by sea, but some came overland, too. *The Granite State & California Mining & Trading Company*, organized in Boston in 1849, had 29 members. The Company "would carry with them and introduce into California New England principles," wrote a member. They travelled with the *Mount Washington Company* and left Boston on Apr. 17, 1849, by Western Railroad and met their president "who had started in advance of the company for the purpose of evading some officers who were in pursuit of him for the object of detaining him until such time as he should be able to liquidate some obligations." They went by Buffalo, Detroit, Chicago, St. Louis, to Independence, from where they set out by mule train. On the 4th of July, on the North Platte, they made as much noise as possible in honor of the day of Independence, as they passed a camp with two large American flags waving above it. By Oct. 18 they reached California and the company disbanded. There, on the Sacramento River they met Capt. Bonner, president of the New Hampshire Temperance Society, who "tapped one of his boat's [whiskey] barrels and commenced drinking the contents." Ah! New England principles! But some remained true. "The New England Society turned out in great force (for the Admission parade) ... Their banner was of superb blue satin, with rich trimmings," with the inscription in gold letters.

RELIGION, LIBERTY & LAW

Sons of the Pilgrims on the Shores of the Pacific

INSTITUTED   OCTOBER 18, 1850~

See K.Webster, *The Gold Seekers of '49*, 1917; and the *Picayune*, Oct. 30, 1850. Before gold was found, New England hadn't wanted this new territory: "Mr. Webster (their chief senator) is for *no* territory," noted Pres. Polk, Feb. 28, 1848. "The Whig Senators ... are opposed to acquiring any territory." - Mar. 3, 1848

"The corporate seal of the City of San Francisco shall bear on its face the arms of the city, representing the Golden Gate in the background, with vessels entering, in the front center a phoenix rising, and on each side emblems of commerce, around the margin the words, 'Seal of the City of San Francisco.' " Nov. 3, 1852. On the flag of 1900 the phoenix is black, the flames gold.

THE SAN FRANCISCO PHOENIX, 1852

Early San Francisco, under our flag, burned up many times. The first great fire began Dec. 24, 1849. High winds and flimsy buildings meant nothing could stop the flames. Yet those who lost their establishments began rebuilding even before the fire was out. On May 4, 1850, a second great fire consumed the rebuilt city; fire bugs were suspected. And again, the city was rebuilt with more energy than before. On June 14, 1850, a third great fire came - just as new buildings were going up as a result of the second fire. This one began in a wooden bakery; the town became a mass of flame. Hook and ladder, and engine companies were formed. Then a fourth great fire began Sept. 17, 1850; sheets of fire again destroyed the city. On May 4, 1851, on the anniversary of the second fire, a fifth great fire began in a paint shop, and was greater than all the earlier fires combined. Even brick buildings fell as wooden roads spread the fire everywhere. All was destroyed, but the ruined citizens set right out to rebuild again. A sixth great fire, which began at Pacific and Powell Streets, came June 22, 1851. This fire had been deliberately set and fierce winds made the flames soar. The next year, the city took the phoenix - who rose from ashes - as its emblem. But it wasn't until 1900 that the phoenix design was used for a city flag, when one was ordered by Mayor Phelan. A motto on a ribbon below the rising bird, from a seal of 1859, stated: "Oro en paz, fierro en guerra" - "Gold in peace, iron in war." Indeed, it was California gold shipped from San Francisco that helped pay for Union iron in the Civil War - and saved the nation.

SEAL OF THE STATE OF CALIFORNIA

The convention which framed the Constitution of the State of California passed a resolution, appropriating $1000 for design for the official Great Seal. One was presented by Mr. Lyons, of which he professed to be the author. It represented the bay of San Francisco as emblematic of the commercial importance of the City and State; with the goddess Minerva, in the foreground, illustrating its sudden springing into maturity; and the Sierra Nevada in the distance, as indicative of the mineral wealth of the country. The motto was the Greek word "Eureka," (εὕρηκα, I have found it.) This was presented to the committee, which consisted virtually of Hon. John McDougal, his associate, Hon. Rodman M. Price, being absent. Gen. McDougal was pleased with the design, and wished it adopted with little or no alteration, but finding that impossible, consented to several minor additions. Thus the figure of the grizzly bear was added, as appropriate to the only section of the country producing the animal. This was especially insisted upon by those who had borne a part in the "Bear Flag" affair. The native Californians opposed it, wrongly supposing that its introduction was intended to immortalize that event. The sheaf of wheat and bunch of grapes were also adopted, as emblems of the agricultural and horticultural interests of the southern sections of the State, particularly. With these exceptions, the seal as designed by Mr. Lyons, was that selected. Soulé, *Annals of San Francisco*, 1855.

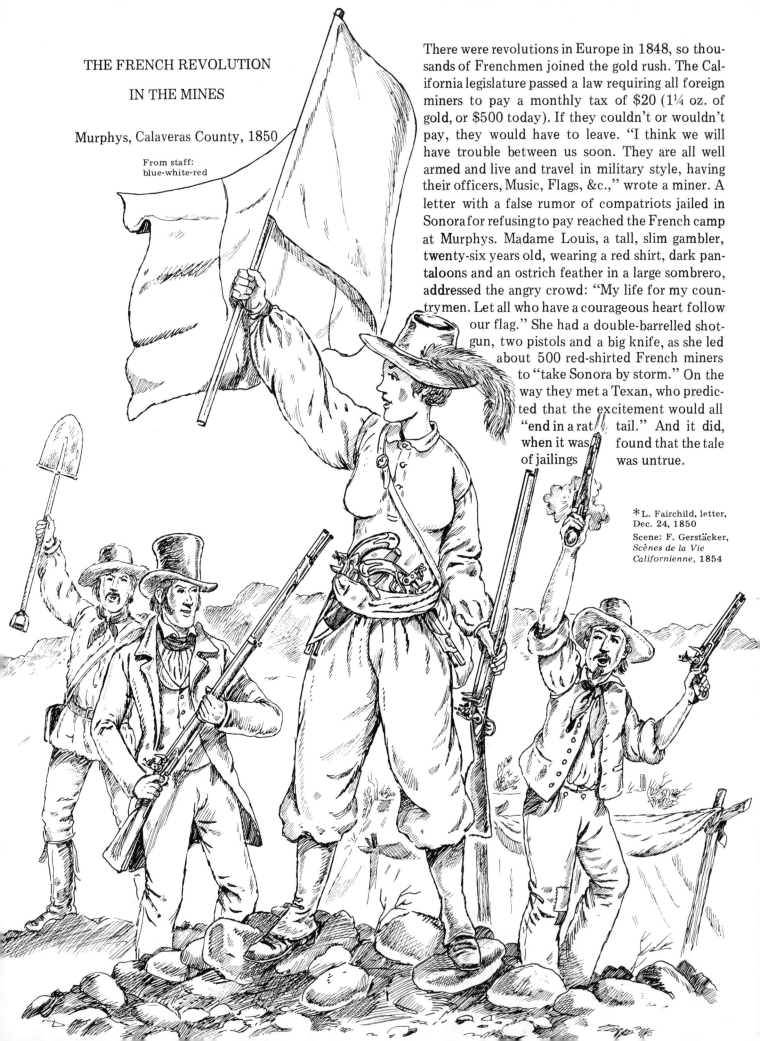

THE FRENCH REVOLUTION
IN THE MINES

Murphys, Calaveras County, 1850

From staff:
blue-white-red

There were revolutions in Europe in 1848, so thousands of Frenchmen joined the gold rush. The California legislature passed a law requiring all foreign miners to pay a monthly tax of $20 (1¼ oz. of gold, or $500 today). If they couldn't or wouldn't pay, they would have to leave. "I think we will have trouble between us soon. They are all well armed and live and travel in military style, having their officers, Music, Flags, &c.," wrote a miner. A letter with a false rumor of compatriots jailed in Sonora for refusing to pay reached the French camp at Murphys. Madame Louis, a tall, slim gambler, twenty-six years old, wearing a red shirt, dark pantaloons and an ostrich feather in a large sombrero, addressed the angry crowd: "My life for my countrymen. Let all who have a courageous heart follow our flag." She had a double-barrelled shotgun, two pistols and a big knife, as she led about 500 red-shirted French miners to "take Sonora by storm." On the way they met a Texan, who predicted that the excitement would all "end in a rat tail." And it did, when it was found that the tale of jailings was untrue.

*L. Fairchild, letter, Dec. 24, 1850
Scene: F. Gerstäcker, *Scènes de la Vie Californienne*, 1854

LE COURIER DE CHERBOURG

AUDACES
FORTUNA
JUVAT

LA CIE. DE LA FORTUNE, PARIS

Few in Europe couldn't stand some quick gold - especially old nobles. Here one Margraff, nephew of the Duke of Baden Baden, raises the flag of the Company of Fortune. He was an old French soldier of the African wars; his bugler had tooted for a cavalry regiment. The military motto means *Fortune Helps the Bold.*

N. Perlot, *Gold Seeker*, Yale, 1985.

THE CALIFORNIA GUARD & THE SAN FRANCISCO POLICE DEPT., 1850

"Aug. 23, the steamer California arrived today with her colors flying at half mast bringing news of the death of President Taylor ... Aug. 29, the funeral procession formed on Broadway ... the California Guard did really make a fine martial appearance - their regimental uniform not yet being furnished, they came out in their fatigue dress, consisting of dark pants and sashes, blue woolen shirts, and a blue cloth military cap ... the city police (further back in the parade, followed), one of the number bearing a large blue satin banner, surmounted by a gilt eagle, appropriately shrouded, on the banner was the following inscription (as shown), in large gold letters ... the banner was beautifully executed ..." Benj. Dore, *Journal* see CHSQ, 1923.

SAN FRANCISCO

POLICE

DEPARTMENT

org. August 12, 1849

THE MARIPOSA BATTALION & THE
DISCOVERY OF YOSEMITE, 1851

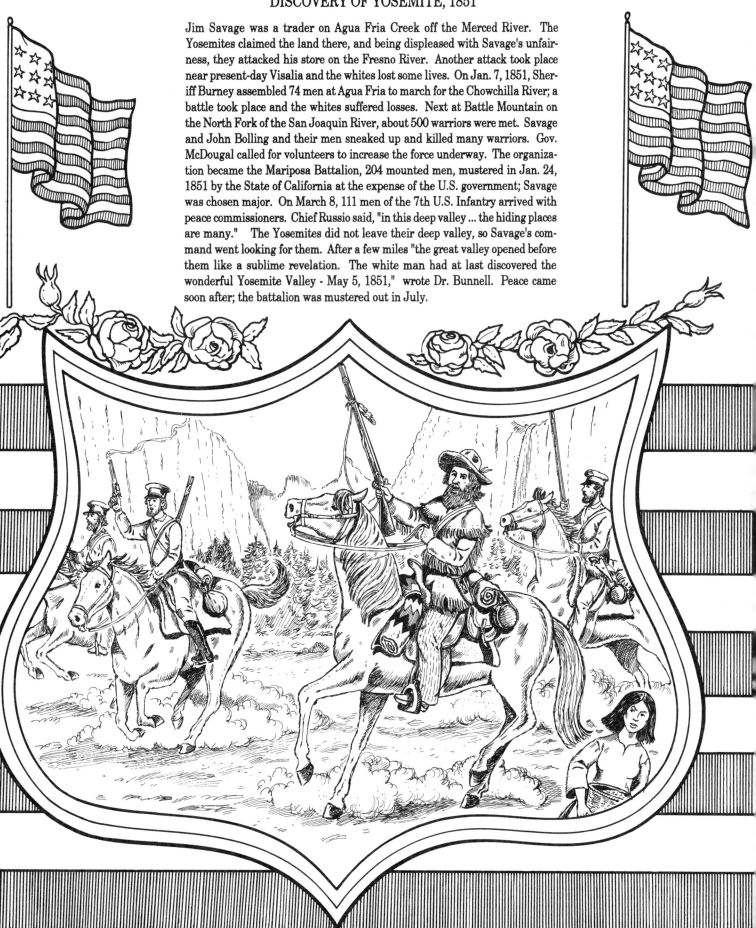

Jim Savage was a trader on Agua Fria Creek off the Merced River. The Yosemites claimed the land there, and being displeased with Savage's unfairness, they attacked his store on the Fresno River. Another attack took place near present-day Visalia and the whites lost some lives. On Jan. 7, 1851, Sheriff Burney assembled 74 men at Agua Fria to march for the Chowchilla River; a battle took place and the whites suffered losses. Next at Battle Mountain on the North Fork of the San Joaquin River, about 500 warriors were met. Savage and John Bolling and their men sneaked up and killed many warriors. Gov. McDougal called for volunteers to increase the force underway. The organization became the Mariposa Battalion, 204 mounted men, mustered in Jan. 24, 1851 by the State of California at the expense of the U.S. government; Savage was chosen major. On March 8, 111 men of the 7th U.S. Infantry arrived with peace commissioners. Chief Russio said, "in this deep valley ... the hiding places are many." The Yosemites did not leave their deep valley, so Savage's command went looking for them. After a few miles "the great valley opened before them like a sublime revelation. The white man had at last discovered the wonderful Yosemite Valley - May 5, 1851," wrote Dr. Bunnell. Peace came soon after; the battalion was mustered out in July.

Flags and shield are from a drawing by R.Eccleston, Bancroft Lib., *Journal of the Mariposa War*, 1957; see also L.Bunnell, *Discovery of the Yosemite*, 1880: "Although ununiformed, they were well armed, and their similarities of dress and accouterments gave them a general military appearance."

VIGILANCE

VANDERBILT LINE
S.S. INDEPENDENCE

CAPTAIN EDGAR WAKEMAN OF THE VIGILANCE NAVY (opposite page), SAN FRANCISCO, JULY 31, 1851

"Executive Committee of the Vigilance Committee to Captain Wakeman ... While our devoted City was undergoing the horrid ordeals of arson, murder & burglaries, when corruption in all Departments of State walked abroad at noon-day, when the people, dismayed and ruined, scarcely knew what to do, I say at that moment you joined the good and virtuous to put down the evils ..." "A beautiful (crimson) satin flag (14 feet long, emblazoned with the words 'Vigilance' and 'Eureka') made by the ladies of San Francisco (was) presented to me ... Such a hurrah with cheers that I never shall forget went up from that crowd of twelve thousand, most of whom had belonged to the Vigilance Committee, and had done good service in clearing society of the most desperate set of villains that ever infested a community. I sailed amid the booming of cannon, saluting the flag." - E. Wakeman

Captain Wakeman's emblem

The Basque Gold Mining Entrepreneur*
THE LEGENDARY SEÑORA MARTINEZ (Mme. Martine), CALAVARAS, 1852

Sonora in Mexico was long fabled for gold and Señora Martinez had been working the placers there - very successfully. Incredibly rich placers were discovered in our Southern mines, and often the locaters just wanted to locate, not work the mines. So Señora Martinez

was sought out to lease the new-found South Carolina Mine, located by Southerners, near Melones, east of Stockton. She brought up a crew of 50 skilled Mexican miners to work for her; she would get 80% of the gold taken out; the lazy locaters would get 20%. The

ore was carried by mules to four arrastras, like the one shown here, for crushing. Soon so much gold was taken out (70,000 oz. in seven months - you figure out what that would be worth , at today's rate of c. $400 an oz.), that the locaters became forlorn - and cancelled the lease when they could. No matter; Señora Martinez made fortunes wherever she went.

Flags of Mexico, from where she & crew came, and France - she was French Basque - fly with O.G. "All the women here dress up like men, for there are no skirts to be seen anywhere." - *Vicente Rosales*, Feb. 1849. Also, "the crowds would make way for the passage of a richly dressed woman ... dashing furiously by, dressed in ... what was quite ... common, male attire." *Annals of S.F.*, 1855, 259.

* Entrepreneurs were dare-devils in olden times. They mixed their cash, credit, pluck and luck to hire people to get some business going. It was a very dangerous sport, and became loathed by the fainthearted unwilling to attempt it. So thousands of little pesky laws were made up to kill off the game. Pity.

To prevent the likes of the Hounds from again taking over and to help maintain order and security, a permanent volunteer military was established. The First California Guard was organized in 1849, of picked young men, veterans of the recent war, full of esprit de corps. In 1850 the Washington Guards were established, and the next year, the Empire Guards of that fire company. Indian disturbances that year added the San Francisco Rangers, the Aldridge Rangers, the Marion Rifle Corps, the Eureka Light Horse Guards, the National Lancers, and the San Francisco Blues. The Sutter Rifles of Sacramento joined the San Francisco companies on July 4, 1853, for a grand review by the venerable and immortal John A. Sutter, who had presented his Rifles with the flag shown.

Everyone knows about John A. Sutter (see our *Rosie & the Bear Flag,* for instance); in the early days he liked to be called the 'Commander of the Fortress of New Helvetia.' The title was none too good for him. A man who fed the hungry, clothed the naked, and comforted the sick. If it's true that Frémont brought the flood of people, old Sutter was there to welcome them."
—*T. Fallon,* Jan. 1, 1881

SUTTER RIFLES
ORGANIZED 26TH JUNE, 1852

THE CALIFORNIA MILITARY COMPANIES

General Sutter's uniform: blue, gold decoration; Captain Fry's uniform: green, red decoration; Flag: probably green, too, and red; See S.F. *Daily Herald,* October 30, 1850, S.F. *Alta,* May 24, 1852

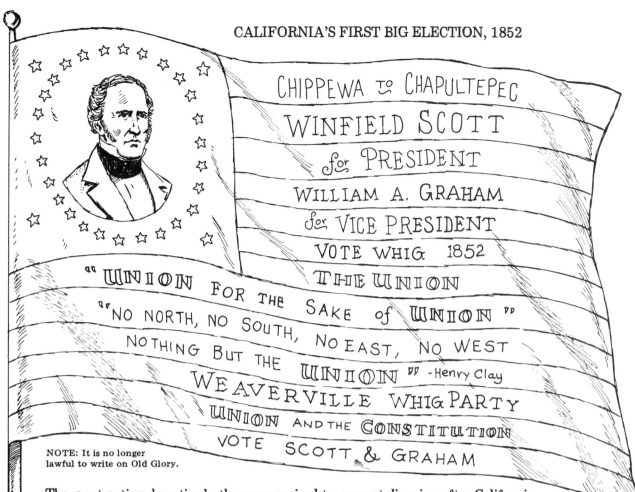

CHIPPEWA to CHAPULTEPEC
WINFIELD SCOTT
for PRESIDENT
WILLIAM A. GRAHAM
for VICE PRESIDENT
VOTE WHIG 1852
THE UNION
"UNION FOR THE SAKE of UNION"
"NO NORTH, NO SOUTH, NO EAST, NO WEST
NOTHING BUT THE UNION" -Henry Clay
WEAVERVILLE WHIG PARTY
UNION AND THE CONSTITUTION
VOTE SCOTT & GRAHAM

NOTE: It is no longer lawful to write on Old Glory.

Note: Gen. Scott was known as "Old Fuss and Feathers" because of his military dress; Mr. Graham was from North Carolina, the "Tar State." Daniel Webster, when he heard of the nomination, labeled it "feathers and tar—tar and feathers," and so Scott was ridiculed and lost the election. Henry Clay and Webster were the great leaders of the Whig Party; both died in 1852, and after this election the party waned away.

The great national parties both compromised to prevent disunion after California was admitted as a free state. The northern Whigs tried to placate the south by nominating a non-political military man, General Scott, for President. The south accepted General Pierce, a northern Democrat, after the election. The Whigs' platform had been subsidies for ships and railroads, lands for farmers and miners. Four years later, the Knownothings, the secretive American Party who were against the foreign born, gathered up the old Whigs and defeated the Democrats. They were also apologists for slavery, so the Republican party was organized in Sacramento by citizens opposed to that vile institution. The few founders included C.P. Huntington, Mark Hopkins, Leland Stanford and the Crockers; their great orator was Colonel Edward Baker—"he rivalled Cicero himself." Buchanan was nominated by the Democrats, Fillmore by the Knownothings, and the Republican flag was Freedom, Frémont and the Railroad. They were opposed by the "Sea-serpent party (Fillmore's), in consideration of its having a fishy smell, being eely and oily and destitute of a backbone... There was only one great national question: whether the general government shall be longer under the control of the slave power. . . or whether it shall subserve the purposes for which our fathers designed it—as a nursery of freedom, and the asylum for the oppressed of all lands—and shall it afford no relief to the oppressed of our own?" The next campaign, 1860, the Democrats split between Douglas (northern) and Breckenridge (southern) and Lincoln was elected. Fort Sumter was fired on on April 12, 1861.

SCOTT FOREVER!

"We have erected a pole 130 feet high with a Scott and Graham flag, of the largest size."
—*Franklin A. Buck*, Weaverville, September 22, 1852

VOTE EARLY!

VOTE OFTEN HUZZAH!

Mining became more difficult, and California was no longer amusing. The Marquis de Pindry, a noble French giant and bear hunter in Contra Costa County, recruited a band of compatriots to colonize the thought-to-be-rich mines of Old Sonora, Mexico. There he was mysteriously murdered. Then a gallant poet-adventurer, the tiny Count Raousset-Boulbon, recruited another army of Frenchmen who were tired of California for the next Sonoran adventure. He captured Hermosillo and soon tried to make Sonora his own independent state. He fell wildly in love with Antonia, the blond daughter of the chief of Altar, an enemy. But the conquest was lost at the Battle of Guaymas. His men were routed; among them were too many lawyers for harmony. The brave count was shot by firing squad on the beach, to the grief of the Sonoran ladies. His adventures had stirred up concern in Washington; the U.S. quickly made the Gadsden Purchase.

INDEPENDANCE DE LA SONORE !

Si, mille fois trompé,
tu conserves la foi,
Si tu luttes encore,
enfant! tu seras roi!

Count Gaston de
RAOUSSET-BOULBON
1853

See A. de Lachapelle,
Le Comte de Raousset-Boulbon, 1859,
p. 120

His coulors were
gold, black and red.
Red shirt.

WILLIAM WALKER THE FILIBUSTER, 1853

Restless Americans were so used to moving on to new territory that they just had to keep looking for more. What Austin had done in Texas, Frémont in California, others could do elsewhere. William Walker opened a recruiting office in San Francisco, announced he was sailing with an army from California to take Sonora. A strong defense awaited him there, so he sailed instead to capture La Paz. The Republic of Lower California was declared by President Walker, but the inhabitants rebelled. Then the capital was moved to bleak Todos Santos, where Walker's men drilled for the Sonoran invasion. The name was changed to the Republic of Sonora, divided into two states, Sonora and Lower California. He expected they would be annexed to the Union as slave states, since he was a southerner. The men didn't enjoy tramping in the desert, though, and many deserted. The few who remained were finally rescued from angry Mexican citizens by the U.S. Army. Walker later appeared in Nicaraugua with another filibuster army, misruled the country, was captured and shot.

Red-blue-red stripes, white stars, gray eyes, blue uniforms

See: Horace Bell, *Reminiscenses of a Ranger*, 1881; A. Woodward, *Repub. of Lower California*, 1966

Vice President Watson

GERMAN CALIFORNIA: THE MAY FESTIVAL OF THE *TURNVEREIN* (GYM CLUB), SAN FRANCISO, 1853

Repressed Germans, in 39 despotic states of Germany, had been prohibited from assembling except for sports. So in the 1810s the *Turnverein* was organized by Friedrich Jahn, to boost fervent German patriotism through sport gatherings. But freedom was otherwise lacking throughout Germany, and in 1821, the new Mexican Emperor Iturbide was about to bring 10,000 German families to California - until he got shot. So it was not until the revolutionary year of 1848 and the Gold Rush that Germans really began to come here. They brought their *Turnverein* and all their enthusiasm for a free and united Germany back home.

The black-red-gold colors of the movement for German unification also represented a cry for liberty. They had been the colors of the Holy Roman Empire.

Flags at the top of California: THE YREKA & HUMBUG VOLUNTEERS, Sept. 10, 1853

In 1853, the fierce Modocs of the Rogue River in southern Oregon, being badly treated by the settlers, decided to even up the score. Capt. Alden's Co. E, 4th U.S. (mounted) Infantry at Fort Jones, Yreka, Siskiyou County, set out to help out. With him went 80 fighting citizen grandees of the Humbug & Yreka mining camps. The ladies there presented two flags to the companies as they rode off.

YREKA
1853
VOLUNTEER CO.

THE HUMBUG VOLUNTEERS
SEPT 10, 1853

All great revolutions were owing to women.

In der Spanierin fand Liebe und Leben ich nur!

Flag: gold crown; white field, blue outer stripes; arms: center shield blue and white; upper right and lower left quarters, red and white; upper left, gold lion, lower right blue lion

Lola, short for Dolores, Montez, born in Ireland, raised in India, Scotland, England and France, was an actress, a dancer and an adventuress—and she conquered King Ludwig I of Bavaria in love. He made her Countess of Landsfeld. "Under her counsels," she wrote, "a total revolution afterwards took place." She supported popular rights and thus "became a fiend, a devil, a she-dragon" to displaced nobility. "The revolution broke out and drove her from power," so in 1852 she came to America and the next year she conquered San Francisco. There she did her Spider Dance, and roars rent the air. She married at Mission Dolores, went to Sacramento and there addressed a boisterous crowd: "You cowards, low blackguards, cringing dogs and lazy fellows!" Tremendous enthusiasm followed. She moved to Grass Valley with her parrot and poodle and found a pet grizzly bear. And there old European plotters talked of making Lola "Empress of California."

THE TUOLUMNE - YOSEMITE WAR, MERCED RIVER, 1854

The French adventurers of the Fortune Co. soon found themselves in a war between the Tuolumnes and the Yosemites over salmon. The old soldiers joined their friends the Yosemites, who sent signals with a flag made of a red shirt on a stick.

Soon peace was made. The French had worked with the Yosemites at gold digging all summer, and took their side in trying to have them restored to their ancient lands. "To push them back would be to exterminate them entirely," for they could find nothing to eat in the snowy mountains. This led to a general peace; all and sundry were ordered to let them be in peace and to protect them.

See J.Perlot, *Gold Seeker*, Yale, 1985

CAPTAIN ULYSSES S. GRANT SERVES AT FORT HUMBOLDT, Jan. 5 - May 7, 1854

Capt. Grant arrived with the 4th U.S. Infantry at San Francisco on the S.S. *Golden Gate* in Aug., 1852. He went then to the army post at Benicia. His regiment left Benicia Sept. 14, 1852 for the Oregon Terrritory. Soon Grant's Co. F was ordered to Fort Humboldt, California, at Bucksport near Eureka; there he remained four months. "It is not true that General Grant was a whiskey guzzler," it was later said. But Capt. Grant fell into trouble with Col. Buchanan: Grant enjoyed frequent visits to Brett's Saloon on First St., Eureka. So he was ordered to Fort Jones, near Yreka, on June 10, 1854, and a month later he resigned from the army. Now he could join his wife Julia and children in Missouri. "I left the Pacific coast very much attached to it, and with the full expectation of making it my future home," he later wrote. But his home became the White House. After his administration, Gen. Grant came back to San Francisco on Sept. 20, 1879. The city gave him a wild welcome. "I was a Confederate soldier," said one, "but God bless you old soul." Another said, "General, since you came to the coast business is better, money is flowing, and people are happier."

WALKER OF YUBA FILIBUSTERS AGAIN, NICARAGUA, 1856

See W.Wells, *Walker's Expedition, 1856*

For he was true
as any star
And brave as Yuba's
grizzlies are.
- *Joaquin Miller*

5 OR NONE

Walker next took an army of Californians to Nicaragua - a crossing place to California. They took Granada, and more Californians came. Pres. Walker improved his flag in Sept., 1856. The old design had five erupting volcanoes representing the Central American countries; the new flag had two blue stripes with a white stripe between, and a red star and the legend "Five or None" representing his prey.

San Francisco in 1848 had 812 inhabitants; by the end of 1849 it had about 18,000. Social conduct there was deplorable: gambling and drinking, fights and brawls were everywhere. Thieves and rapscallions came to town in large numbers. Many of them were hardened old English convicts from the penal colonies in Australia who claimed that enough more were coming from there to take over. Late in '49 and in the '50s, San Francisco had a series of terrible fires which demolished the city; they were thought to have been purposely set. Justice was weak, so the famous Vigilance Committee was formed in 1851 to preserve lives and property. One Jenkins committed "a vile depredation" on June 10 and was directly hanged by the citizens. Then an old English villain, James Stuart, from Sydney, was caught. He confessed a myriad of crimes and was hung. Two more villains, Whittaker and MacKensie, met the same end. Evil-doers left town. In August, the Vigilance Committee,

with 700 members, suspended its operations. By 1855 there were about 75,000 people in San Francisco, and many were wild and bad. On November 18, General Richardson, the U.S. Marshal, was assassinated by Charles Cora, a fancy-dressing gambler, who was quickly arrested. Soon the old Vigilance Committee bell sounded. Cora, with eminent and able lawyers, was tried, but the jury reached no verdict. Then another crime took place on May 14, 1856: James Casey, editor of the *Sunday Times*, shot James King, editor of the *Evening Bulletin*. Members of the Vigilance Committee met and organized anew. Soon they numbered 2,600 men, organized into companies of 100. They were directed by Charles Doane from headquarters at 41 Sacramento Street. The Citizens' Guard, sixty picked men led by Captain Olney, escorted the companies as they all marched off to the jail on Broadway to take Casey. A cannon was placed before the door. "I will go with them," said Casey, seeing no other way. Cora's presence was also requested. King died on May 19; Casey and Cora met their ends during his funeral, dangling from the second floor of the Vigilance Committee headquarters. "My faults are the result of my early education," said Casey. Two more bad fellows, Hetherington and Brace, were also hung. Then, on August 21, before disbanding, the Vigilance Committee held a parade on Third Street. By then there were four infantry regiments each with its own colors, two cavalry squadrons, battalions of artillery, riflemen, pistolmen, and police—over 6,000 men. Olney had become Brigadier General of all. The huge banner of the first Vigilance Committee was in a place of honor.

BATTALION
CITIZENS GUARD

COMM   E OF VIGIL

THE VIGILANCE
COMMITTEE

1851 and 1856

"It is an extremely serious thing for any organized community to throw over the orderly methods slowly and painfully developed through a thousand years of civilization, in the effort to rectify by violence the inefficacy or corruption of officials of its own choice, who can in our country always be changed with but little delay by safe and legal methods devised for the purposes."

—*General Wistar*

The 1851 Banner, on the wagon, presented by the Ladies of Trinity Church, was lost in 1906. It was made of blue satin with gilt lettering, shaded with darker blue and red. The banner of the Citizens Guard is shown minutely in a contemporary letter sheet. Black uniforms. See *Military Gazette*, August 30, 1856.

Scandinavian California:
JOHN SNOWSHOE THOMPSON,
THE NORWEGIAN HERO, DREAMS OF
HOME WHILE CARRYING THE MAIL, 1856

CARSON-PLACERVILLE EXPRESS

Snowshoe arrived in California in 1851, to get some gold. He then ranched on Putah Creek - today U.C. Davis - and in 1855 he made a set of skis, then called "snowshoes," 10ft. long and 25 pounds of oak. In January, 1856, he first went by ski from Placerville to Genoa, Carson Valley, Nevada Territory - 90 miles with 40 pounds of mail; he made the trip in four days. He soon made the trip weekly, sometimes with over 100 pounds of mail, and he was never lost, no matter how fierce the storms. The miners along the route thought snowshoeing looked like fun, and many soon tried it. Races were held in the 1850s, and skiing fast became the major sport in the Sierras. In February 1869, Snowshoe and his Alpine Boys were defeated by the Sierra Boys, who greased their skis. Snowshoe carried the winter mail for almost twenty years, over many difficult, dangerous passes. He saved lives on his cross-country journeys, too.

Flag of United Norway and Sweden, 1814-1905: top and bottom - red field, white outer cross, blue center cross; sides - light blue field, gold cross. See the *Overland Monthly*, Oct. 1886, and R.Power, *Pioneer Skiing in Cal.*, 1960

"The miners on Jack Ass Flat & Horsetown made a strike for cheaper water - price 75 cents per inch - which they the miners want three inches for a dollar. So on this day they marched en masse into Shasta City about 600 in number. Several banners floated gaily o'er our heads." - Joaquin Miller, *Diary*. The water was from the new Big Ditch, about one hundred miles long.

A miner's inch = 9 gals. per minute.

ADAMS & CO'S

DRUGS

WATER
!!
!!

CHEAP WATER !

JACK ASS FLAT 3 for $ HORSETOWN

HOTEL

WASHIN

CALIFORNIA & WATER: SHASTA, MAY 22, 1856

MRS. PATTEN, 19, SAILS
NEPTUNE'S CAR INTO
SAN FRANCISCO
November, 15 1856

Captain Patten, 29, had brain fever and the first mate was in the brig for badness. Mrs. Patten took command of the fast clipper ship, for she was expert at seamanship. In spite of lying 80 days off Cape Horn in terrible seas, she reached San Francisco in 136 days - a good time considering the foul weather.

Flag of Coleman's Line: Vertical lines = red; horizontal lines = blue.

Texas and California had been taken by filibusters, and Southerners were looking for more states. Henry Crabb was bored in the legislature in Sacramento. He had a wife from Sonora, and stealing the real estate there still seemed a good idea - despite Walker's fiasco. Crabb gathered up an army in California of 96 adventurers, called the "Arizona Colonization Company," and took them to Yuma, and on April 1, 1857, they went over the border to Caborca. "I have come with the intention of injuring no one," said Crabb. But Gov. Pesqueira knew better: "Show no mercy to these hounds, this accursed horde of pirates," he said. "Death to the Filibusters." Crabb's army marched along, when "bang!" From behind the walls came the fire. Crabb returned the fire. The Mexicans then occupied their lovely

Flag: "Haced que nuestra bandera, sublime creación del genio de Iguala, sea llevada alto, muy alto. Haced que en ella se escriban las palabras: LIBERTAD O MUERTE." - Pesqueira, *Voz de Sonora*, Mar. 30, 1857.

church. Crabb and fifteen men ran across the plaza to storm the church and a keg of powder was put before the door. But the men were getting killed and the powder didn't go off. Then the Mexicans charged, and Crabb was shot and retreated. The Mexicans put artillery in front of the Americans' position, and set the roof on fire. Crabb surrendered.

FREE SPEECH, FREE PRESS, FREE SOIL, FREE MEN

FREMONT AND VICTORY & THE RAILROAD

Lincoln gave ninety speeches for Frémont. "Frémont & Jessie" seemed to be the Republican ticket, and "the women of the North enlisted under Frémont's banner as they had never before enlisted in politics." *Don* Pío Pico urged Californians to vote for Frémont. But he was beaten by a few Whig and Know-Nothing votes for Buchanan and Fillmore. Yet he fixed public sentiment in the North on the slavery question, and Lincoln would pick up the banner next. Frémont went back to California.

We'll give 'em Jessie,
We'll give 'em Jessie,
We'll give 'em Jessie,
When we rally at the polls.

Fremont and Dayton

Flag: Smithsonian Institute.

THE KNOW-NOTHINGS, 1855

Clay and Webster were dead, and their Whig Party was dissolving; the secret American Party took its place. Hostility to recently arrived immigrants was its cause. The party got its name due to its members who, when asked about their party, always said they knew nothing about it. In 1855 the entire K-N ticket was elected in California. They supported Fillmore for president in 1856 and helped defeat Frémont. The K-Ns broke up in 1857. Frémont's party remained.

LIBERTY

K. N.

AMERICAN PARTY

Banner: from the K-N Quick Step, 1854; the raccoon was the symbol of the Whigs, the rooster of the Democrats.

Frémont bought the Mariposa Ranch from Alvarado in 1847, 70 sq. miles and 43,000 acres for $3,000; and gold was shortly discovered there. "The Hornitas (a place of evil fame) League, 'the terror of the neighborhood,' jumped the Black Drift;" the Merced Mining Co. had sent a small army of "the most noted criminals of the county" to seize the Frémonts' richest mine. The sheriff refused to do his duty; the besiegers attempted to starve out the Frémont men from the mine - an unoccupied state was required to take possession. "But," reported Jessie, "little Mrs. Ketton took a revolver and a basket of provisions and presented herself at the mouth of the mine - they refused her entrance. She said she would go & pushed on & told them if they 'offered to touch her, she'd fire' & if she fired our men would have rushed in & fired also & at the same time they would all have been blown up for the men in the drift had laid ... blasting powder near the entrance & were ready to do their part ... they let her in & after that she went in twice daily, carrying food in her hands & under her clothes pistols & powder & caps." Gov. Weller sent the military companies at Columbia, Sonora & Stockton, and, Jessie continued, "friends in San Francisco have sent me up 100 muskets with bayonets & abundance of ammunition ... this is a great triumph. Coulterville had lately raised and equipped a uniformed Home Guard, and this body volunteered to march over at once. The game was up. In a brief time all was again safely back in smooth working order, even the Black Drift." - *Jessie Benton Frémont*, Bear Valley, July 18, 1858

JESSIE FRÉMONT IN COMMAND, THE MARIPOSA WAR, 1858

Hell's Hollow, Bear Valley:
Bad ground for a Fight!

COULTERVILLE GUARD

STOCKTON GUARDS

Lt. Edw. BEALE
& the U.S. Camel Corps,
1857

US
K

Jeff Davis became Sec. of War in 1853, and he thought camels ideal for crossing the deserts of the new territory acquired from Mexico. So camels were bought at Tunis and brought to Texas, where from Fort Defiance Edward Beale led an expedition of 24 dromedary camels to Fort Tejon in California, to look over the road for a mail route. Near Fort Davis, Texas, with some U.S. dragoons, they camped where soldiers had been killed battling fierce natives. The road between El Paso and Sante Fé was the dread and terror of all travellers. At San Elizario the inhabitants became wildly amazed over the camels - animals never before seen. The "economical and noble brute" won Beale's praise; "our admiration for them increased day by day," he said. Two of the camels arrived at Los Angeles on November 10, 1857; 14 more camels appeared there on January 8.

Red & white guidon.

BODIE, MINING TOWN IN THE SKY, ELEV. 8300'

"... her gold mines are the most wonderful yet discovered," - the first telegram out.

Wm. Bodey, a New York Dutchman, came to Cal. in 1848. He was out prospecting, in 1859, and found gold up on the barren eastern slope of the Sierra Nevada, north of Mono Lake. Then Bodey got lost in a blizzard, which ended his career. A quartz mine began there that year and a sign painter changed the spelling of the place to Bodie. The Bodie Bluffs Consolidated Mining Co. was formed in 1863, with Gov. Stanford a part owner - and he declared it worthless. The company's Standard Mine passed into the hands of Bill O'Hara, a black gent who ran a boarding house and got the mine for back rent. O'Hara, here, offered easy terms to anyone who'd run the mine. Soon the operators who had given up before came back, and then - boom! An earthquake opened up a huge golden vien, the Fortuna Ledge. The Standard Mine then sold for a fat price, and the buyers became really rich. But Bodie is famous not just for gold, but for the bad men and wild girls who went there.

This gorgeous flag is still in the Bodie Miners Union Hall. See Ellen Cain, *Bodie*, 1956.

BODIE MINERS' UNION.

BODIE MINER'S UNION ORGANIZED DEC 22ND 187-

Good-by, God! I'm going to Bodie."

The place became known as "Shooters' Town," with killings nightly, it seemed. Half the mile long main street consisted of saloons. There were seven breweries. A vigilance committee - the "601" - kept very busy, but murders didn't let up. Paid gunmen fought over claims; stage robbers held up gold shipments; and, liquor loosened trigger fingers, generally. Happily, Bodie today is a most interesting State Park.

IRISH CALIFORNIA

Irishmen came early to California. Timothy Murphy was here in 1828, settled at San Rafael in 1836 and hunted over the countryside with his hounds. Father Short came from Hawaii in 1832 and taught at Hartnell's school near Monterey. In 1845 Father McNamara asked the president of Mexico for a huge grant of land in California for an Irish colony of 10,000 souls. Otherwise, he said, "Your Excellency may be assured that before another year the Californias will form a part of the American union." And sure enough: the Stars and Stripes were soon flying everywhere. It was claimed later that a reason for the Bear Flag Revolt was to prevent McNamara from succeeding. The failures of the Irish potato crops of 1845-9 caused huge numbers of Irish folk to come to the United States in the '50s— 221,253 in 1851 alone. Many came to California and stayed. A beautifully painted flag led their procession to the mission in San Francisco on St. Patrick's Day, 1854.

THE PONY EXPRESS, next page

News was everything, and it had been coming to California from the East via Panama Steamer—a long, round-about way. Then in 1858, stages of Butterfield's Overland Mail came twice a week by way of 165 stations, on the wide sweep out of the way of the Southern Route, 19 days from Missouri to California, about the same time as the mail took on the steamers. Butterfield had a subsidy of $600,000 a year from the government, which was southern-controlled and opposed to any shorter, quicker northern route. William Russell's great Pony Express, the "Central Overland California and Pikes Peak Express Co.," was chartered without government money, and with fresh horses every 10-12 miles, begun on April 3, 1860, with William Richardson galloping westward. Each rider would change at least three horses and ride 75-100 miles; delivery was promised within 13 days from Missouri. A mochilla with four cantinas filled with mail was thrown over the saddle and quickly changed at each relay. The Express arrived at Placerville April 15. There, Bill Hamilton grabbed the mochilla from Warren Upson. He was delayed by a grand reception with bands and waving flags, but soon on he raced and reached Sacramento at 5:25 that day. There a celebration long remembered burst forth. Hamilton was met by Capt. Eyre's Sacramento Hussars, who rode furiously ahead of him from Sutter's Fort to J Street. From Sacramento the Pony Express went by the fast steamboat *Antelope* to San Francisco, where he arrived at 11:30 to shooting rockets and more cheers and the California Band playing "See the Conquering Hero Comes." The Fire Companies in their colorful uniforms escorted Hamilton and his gaily decorated pony, now wearing a woman's expensive bonnet, in a torch-lit parade to the *Alta Telegraph* office, the end of the trip. Soon, Sibley's Pacific and Overland Telegraph Companies—with government money—completed a wire to California on October 24, 1861. The last ride of the pony was near. Before long, the northern-controlled Congress would finance the Central Pacific Rail Road where the pony had ridden.

You know the color.
Annals of San Francisco, p. 524

THE PONY EXPRESS ARRIVES AT SACRAMENTO, 5:25 P.M., APRIL 15, 1860

THE FIRST CALIFORNIA GUARD (Flying Artillery), "The Pioneer Corps of California," 1860

Colors: "The Company shall have two Silken colors and a silken guidon, the first on the National color of Stars and Stripes, the name of the Company to be embroidered with gold on the centre stripe. The second to be yellow, bearing in the centre two cannon crossing, with the letters, F.C.G. above, and the figure 1, below; fringe, yellow." Coat: dark blue, collar and cuffs of scarlet cloth, near the front a shell and flame of yellow metal; on each shoulder a scarlet worsted epaulette, secured by shoulder straps to be edged with gold braid; the front seams, seams of skirts and cuffs, to be edged with red cloth. Cap: dark blue cloth, band at the lower edge of the cap of scarlet cloth with an ornament in front of cross cannon of yellow metal; a red horse-hair plume to be worn with yellow metal spread eagle; the band to be edged with gold braid. Gilt buttons the same as for officers of artillery, USA with the letter A on the shield. Trousers: of white and light blue mixed cloth, commonly called "Army blue," with a stripe of scarlet cloth on each side, the stripe to be edged with gold braid. Chevrons of gold.

Bill of Dress, July 27, 1860

On July 27, 1849, in San Francisco at the school house on the plaza, 41 gentlemen organized an artillery corps (though they would also train with muskets) to be known as the "First California Guard." The army had been "inefficient," and the officers of the law needed help. Soon after this, many other guard units were formed, too. Here, the Guard are in the uniforms of 1860. "Although we have no State Military Academy, San Francisco possesses a military school—the Old Guard—the First California Guard . . May she prove the West Point of California."* When the Civil War came, men of the Guard joined the California One Hundred, or California "Rangers," whom we will see presently. The Guard also provided soldiers for the Confederacy.

The Paiutes were peaceable until the Williams brothers waylaid their girls. Then they did bloody justice, whereupon Major Ormsby and 106 white avengers met the Indians at Pyramid Lake. There, young Chief Winnemucca outsoldiered Ormsby, who lost most of his men. Panic flew over the hills to California, and an army of a thousand hurried to the rescue.

Dark blue coats with light blue collars and cuffs; dark blue caps with light blue bands around bases; light blue pompon, epaulets on soldiers; gold epaulets on officer; light blue trousers with gold stripes. Brass buttons and belt plates. Brass eagle cap insignias.

THE PAIUTE WAR, 1860

THE SIERRA GUARD BATTALION

ORG. SEPT. 30, 1854

RE-ORG. MAR 24, 1856

DOWNIEVILLE

SIERRA GUARD BN. CALIFORNIA MILITIA

Murphy, of Colonel Daniel Hungerford, 1891

From Downieville came Major Hungerford with his Sierra infantry battalion. Col. Jack Hays, mentioned before, was Commander-in-Chief of all. The big battle soon happened, and Major Hungerford, "...was able to save the day. Were it not for the discipline of his men, and his tactical manoeuvring . . . every man in the command would have been massacred. The well-conceived plan of young Winnemucca, the intelligent chief," was perceived. The Indians escaped to the Truckee River.

THE
CALIFORNIA
MILITARY COMPANIES:
The Emmett Home Guard,
c. 1860

When the Vigilance Committee roared into action in 1856, all of the military companies in San Francisco broke up because few members would oppose the V.C. After the committee retired, some new companies formed: the Black Hussars - abolitionists - and the California Fusiliers, 1857; the Light Guard, 1858; the French Guard and McMahon Guard, 1859. Then came the civil war and many of the men were soon wearing Federal blue or Confederate gray. Here is another Irish company from just before the war. The independent companies became the State militia and in time the idea led to the formation of the National Guard Companies of California.

Erin go Unum
E Pluribus bragh.
- *Phoenix*

Flag: green; Emmett's flag uniform, dark green. Uniforms: green jackets, blue trousers, gilt buttons, braid and busby plate. White belting. From *The Military of San Francisco*, pub. by G.Baker, 408 Cal. St., 1871

See E. Kennedy, *The Contest for Cal. in 1861*, 1912

HONEST ABE

A Very Great Moment in California politics: COLONEL BAKER, the new U.S. Senator from Oregon (& just from California) speaking in San Francisco for his lifetime friend Abe Lincoln, The American Theatre, Friday, Oct. 26, 1860. Young Bret Harte, carried away, leapt on stage with Old Glory. Speaking for Freedom & the Republican Party, Baker gave "what was supposed to be the greatest speech ever delivered in California." - *Hittell*

THE UNION!

"I will not be false to freedom. I know her power. I glory in her strength. I rejoice in her majesty. I will walk beneath her banner ... the genius of America will at last lead her sons to freedom."
— *E. Baker*

His speech went to every corner of California, and won the state for Lincoln.

"O brothers by the farther sea!
Think still our faith is warm;
The same bright flag above us waves
That swathed our baby form."
— *Bret Harte*

THE GREAT SEAL WHEN CALIFORNIA BECAME A PART OF THE U.S.A.

Enlarged from the Die of 1841 of the Great Seal used under President Polk, made by John Throop.

For the amazing history of this delightful emblem, you will surely want THE STORY OF OUR FLAG, profusely illustrated and as never before, just $3.95 at your store or merely add $2.50 for shipping and write us.